Howard Chandler Christy

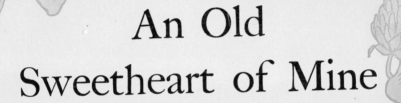

An Old Sweetheart of Mine

James Whitcomb Riley

Drawings by

Howard Chandler Christy

Decorations by
Virginia Keep

The Bobbs-Merrill Company
Publishers   Indianapolis

PRESS OF
BRAUNWORTH & CO.
BOOKBINDERS AND PRINTERS
BROOKLYN, N. Y.

INSCRIBED

To GEORGE C. HITT

The beginning of whose steadfast friendship was marked by the first publication of these verses which now, expanded by writer, honored by publisher and masterfully graced by artist, seem to be a worthier symbol of the author's grateful and affectionate regard for his earliest friend

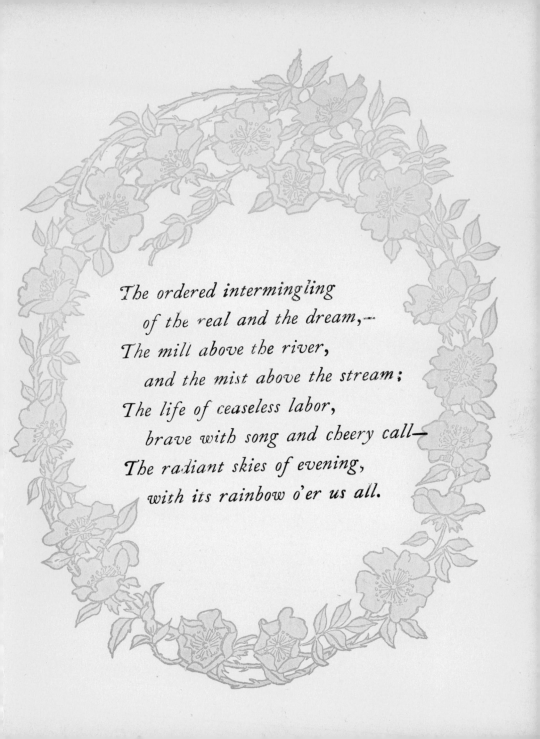

The ordered intermingling
　　of the real and the dream,—
The mill above the river,
　　and the mist above the stream;
The life of ceaseless labor,
　　brave with song and cheery call—
The radiant skies of evening,
　　with its rainbow o'er us all.

AN OLD SWEETHEART OF MINE!—Is this
    her presence here with me,
Or but a vain creation of
    a lover's memory?

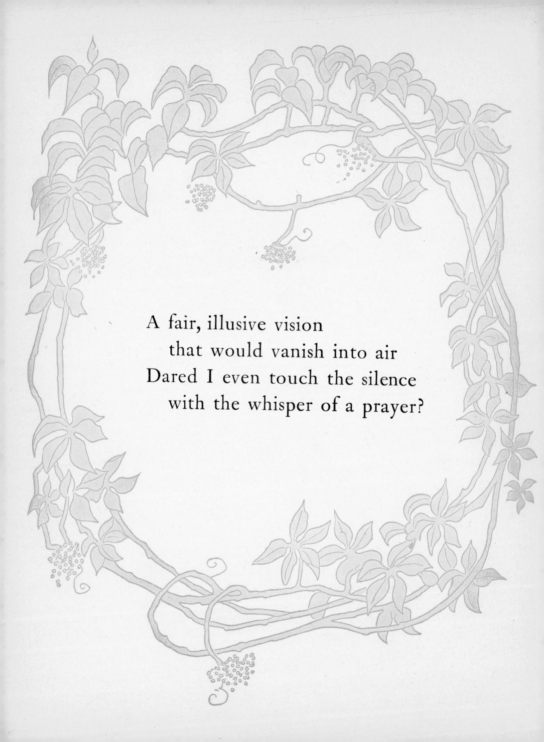

A fair, illusive vision
that would vanish into air
Dared I even touch the silence
with the whisper of a prayer?

Howard Chandler Christy 1902.

Nay, let me then believe in all
the blended false and true—
The semblance of the *old* love
and the substance of the *new*,—

Howard Chandler Christy 1902

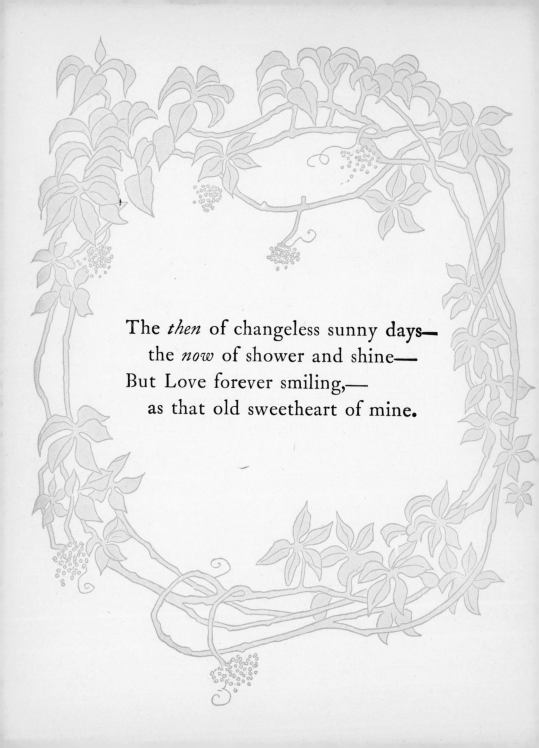

The *then* of changeless sunny days—
   the *now* of shower and shine—
But Love forever smiling,—
   as that old sweetheart of mine.

This ever-restful sense of *home*,
　　though shouts ring in the hall.—
The easy-chair—the old bookshelves
　　and prints along the wall;

The rare *Habanas* in their box,
or gaunt churchwarden-stem
That often wags, above the jar,
derisively at them.

As one who cons at evening
    o'er an album, all alone,
And muses on the faces
    of the friends that he has known,

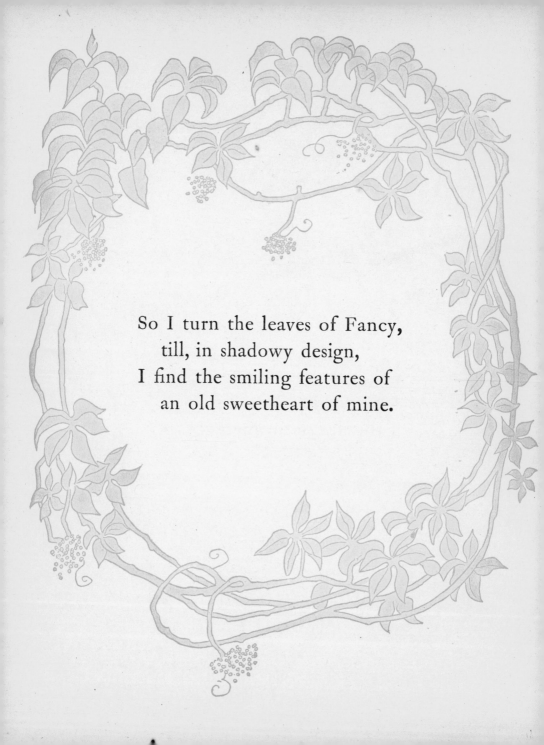

So I turn the leaves of Fancy,
    till, in shadowy design,
I find the smiling features of
    an old sweetheart of mine.

The lamplight seems to glimmer
with a flicker of surprise,
As I turn it low—to rest me
of the dazzle in my eyes,

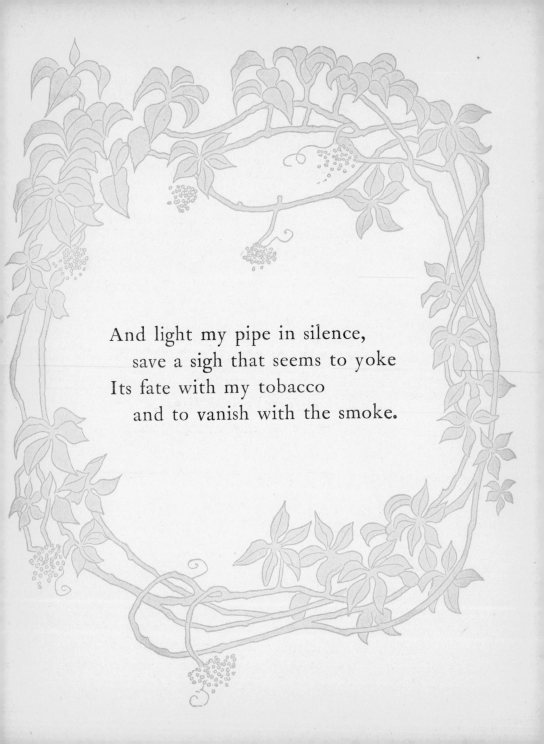

And light my pipe in silence,
    save a sigh that seems to yoke
Its fate with my tobacco
    and to vanish with the smoke.

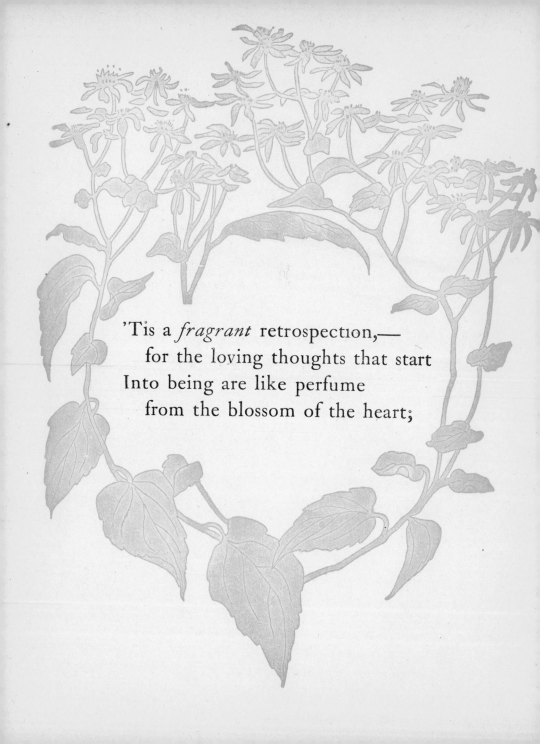

'Tis a *fragrant* retrospection,—
for the loving thoughts that start
Into being are like perfume
from the blossom of the heart;

Howard Chandler Christy 1902

And to dream the old dreams over
is a luxury divine—
When my truant fancies wander
with that old sweetheart of mine.

Though I hear beneath my study,
    like a fluttering of wings,
The voices of my children
    and the mother as she sings—

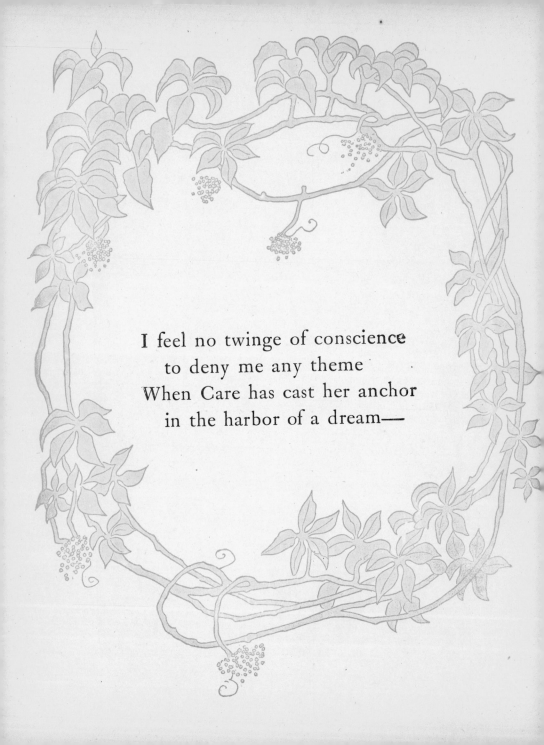

I feel no twinge of conscience
to deny me any theme
When Care has cast her anchor
in the harbor of a dream—

In fact, to speak in earnest,
    I believe it adds a charm
To spice the good a trifle
    with a little dust of harm,—

Howard Chandler Christy · 1905

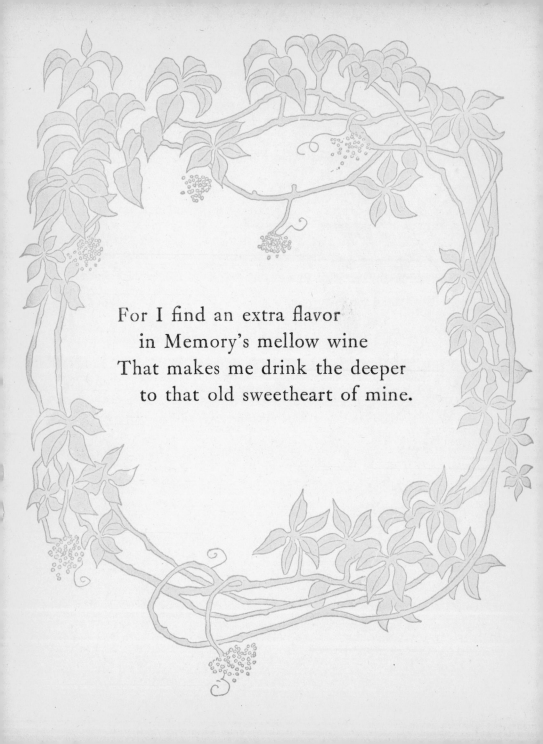

For I find an extra flavor
in Memory's mellow wine
That makes me drink the deeper
to that old sweetheart of mine.

O Childhood-days enchanted!
   O the magic of the Spring!—
With all green boughs to blossom white,
   and all bluebirds to sing!

When all the air, to toss and quaff,
    made life a jubilee
And changed the children's song and
    laugh to shrieks of ecstasy.

With eyes half closed in clouds that ooze
    from lips that taste, as well,
The peppermint and cinnamon,
    I hear the old School-bell,

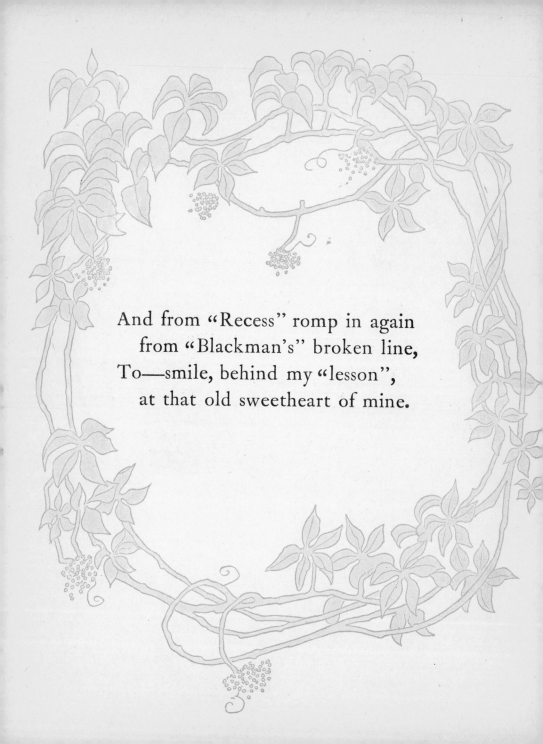

And from "Recess" romp in again
   from "Blackman's" broken line,
To—smile, behind my "lesson",
   at that old sweetheart of mine.

A face of lily-beauty,
    with a form of airy grace,
Floats out of my tobacco
    as the "Genii" from the vase;

And I thrill beneath the glances
of a pair of azure eyes
As glowing as the summer
and as tender as the skies.

I can see the pink sunbonnet
　　and the little, checkered dress
She wore when first I kissed her
　　and she answered the caress

With the written declaration that,
   "As surely as the vine
Grew 'round the stump," she loved me—
   that old sweetheart of mine.

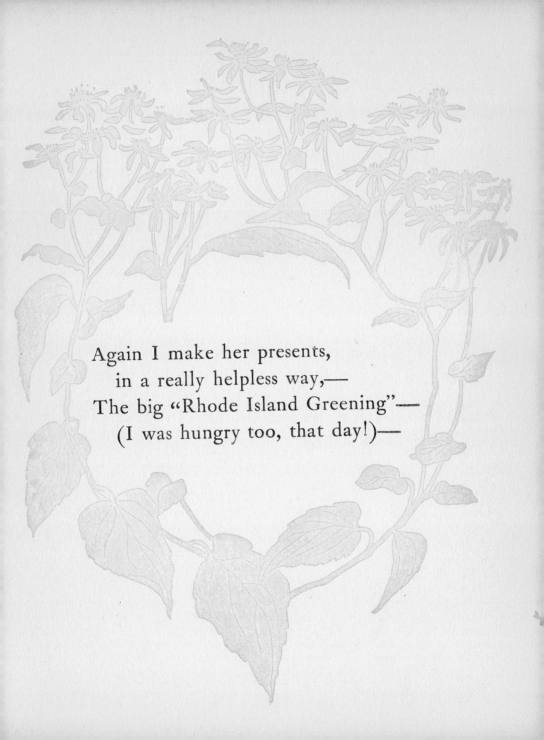

Again I make her presents,
    in a really helpless way,—
The big "Rhode Island Greening"—
    (I was hungry too, that day!)—

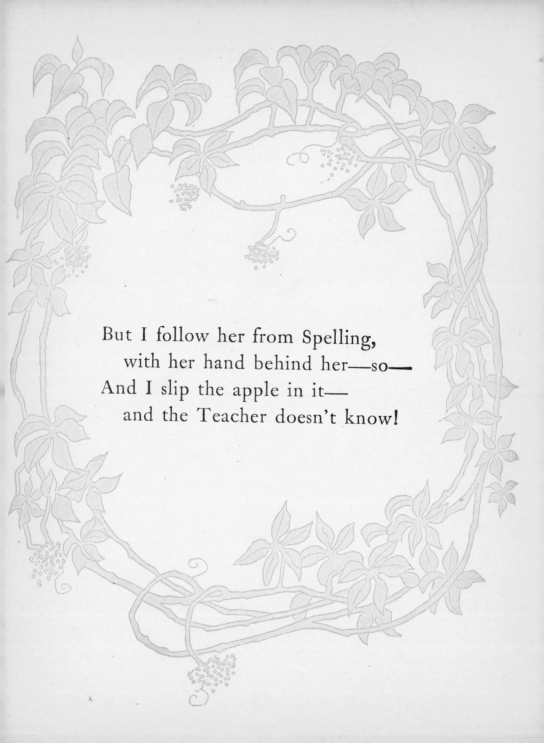

But I follow her from Spelling,
    with her hand behind her—so—
And I slip the apple in it—
    and the Teacher doesn't know!

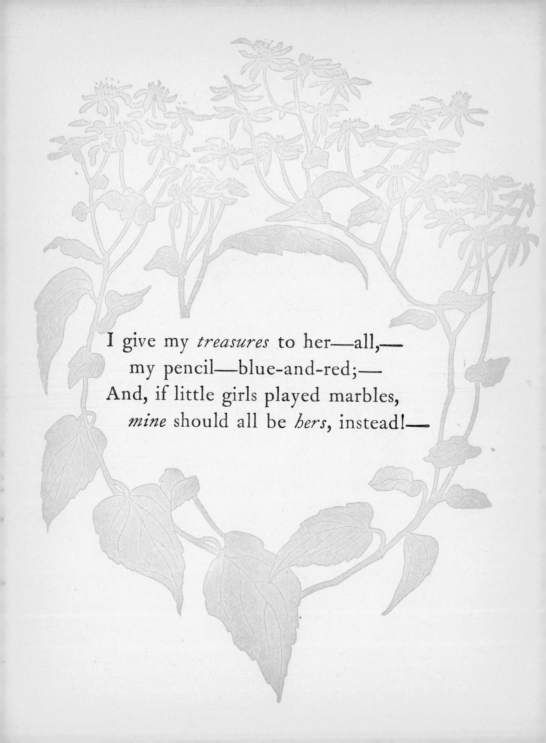

I give my *treasures* to her—all,—
    my pencil—blue-and-red;—
And, if little girls played marbles,
    mine should all be *hers*, instead!—

But *she* gave me her *photograph*,
  and printed "Ever Thine"
Across the back—in blue-and-red—
  that old sweetheart of mine!

And again I feel the pressure
of her slender little hand,
As we used to talk together
of the future we had planned,—

When I should be a poet,
 and with nothing else to do
But write the tender verses
 that she set the music to....

When we should live together
   in a cozy little cot
Hid in a nest of roses,
   with a fairy garden-spot,

Where the vines were ever fruited
and the weather ever fine,
And the birds were ever singing
for that old sweetheart of mine....

When I should be her lover
forever and a day,
And she my faithful sweetheart
till the golden hair was gray;

And we should be so happy
    that when either's lips were dumb
They would not smile in Heaven
    till the other's kiss had come.

Howard Chandler Christy 1912

But, ah! my dream is broken
   by a step upon the stair,
And the door is softly opened,
   and—my wife is standing there:

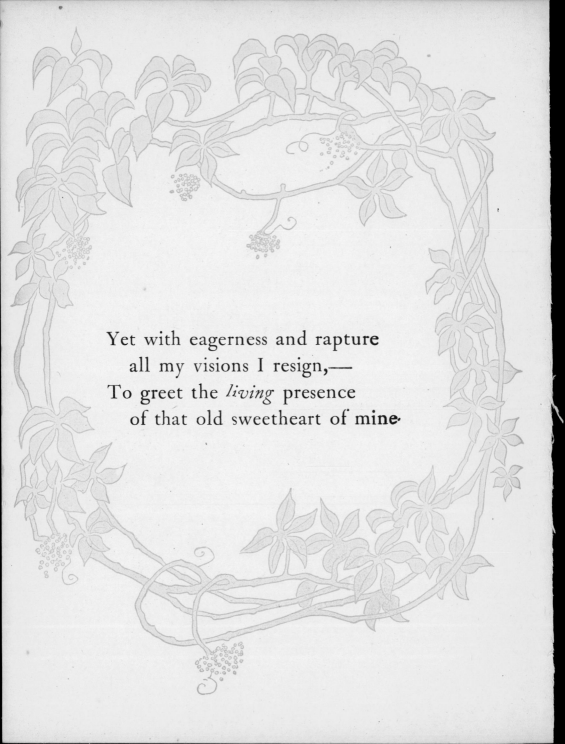

Yet with eagerness and rapture
all my visions I resign,—
To greet the *living* presence
of that old sweetheart of mine·